Distinctive Features of the PRACTICAL ENGLISH WORKBOOK,
Third Edition

Organization

-Parallels the organization of the PRACTICAL ENGLISH HANDBOOK,
Seventh Edition

-Major parts cover grammar, sentence errors, sentence struc-
ture, punctuation, mechanics, diction, and style

-Expanded instructional material introduces a set of exercises
covering each skill

-Many carefully chosen examples of grammar and usage--followed
by full explanations of why the examples are correct or incorrect

-Cross-referenced to PRACTICAL ENGLISH HANDBOOK (see last page
of PRACTICAL ENGLISH WORKBOOK)

Style and Content

-Writing style is concise and readable

-Calls student's attention to distinctions between formal and
informal usage, standard and substandard English, and problems of
style, such as choppy sentences and excessive coordination

-Stresses grammatical correctness in writing as an aid to
reader's understanding, for example, confusion caused by imprecise
pronouns

-Stresses use of dictionary as a writer's key tool

-Covers problems of incorrect idioms, triteness, and wordiness

-Discusses vocabulary building, connotation, figurative and
flowery language

-Emphasizes careful sentence construction including parallel-
ism, variety in sentences, and correct position of modifiers

-Calls attention to details of mechanics--how to handle
apostrophes, hyphenation, abbreviation, numbers

Approach

-Follows a traditional approach to grammar, punctuation, and
syntax as a proven method of improving English skills

-Stresses basic and recurrent problems

-Emphasizes building skills

Instructor's Manual

PRACTICAL ENGLISH WORKBOOK
Third Edition

Instructor's Manual

PRACTICAL ENGLISH WORKBOOK
Third Edition

Floyd C. Watkins
Emory University

William B. Dillingham
Emory University

John T. Hiers
Valdosta State College

HOUGHTON MIFFLIN COMPANY   BOSTON

Dallas   Geneva, Illinois
Lawrenceville, New Jersey   Palo Alto

Grateful acknowledgment is made to the following publishers and
authors for permission to reprint from their works:

William A. Henry, "Journalism Under Fire." Copyright 1983 Time Inc.
All rights reserved. Reprinted by permission from Time.

Norman Myers, "By Saving Wild Species, We May Be Saving Ourselves."
Originally published in the Nov./Dec. TNC News. Reprinted by permission of The Nature Conservancy News.

John Rockwell, "Blues, and Other Noises, in the Night." © 1976
Saturday Review magazine. Reprinted by permission.

Printed in the U.S.A.
ISBN: 0-395-36402-7
ABCDEFGHIJ-A-93210/998765

CONTENTS

CONTENTS

CONTENTS

CONTENTS

1.1 Nouns

1. societies; restoration; buildings

2. excavations; accounts; era; Solomon

3. atlases; guides; travelers

4. cereals; protein

5. century; factories; United States; supply; mussels

6. veterinarians; acupuncture; value; treatment; animals

7. Galapagos Islands; origin; Pacific Ocean; wonders

8. selenium; doses; part; diet

9. laws; vaccination; rabies; dogs; cats

10. engineering; agriculture; mining; medicine

1.2 Pronouns

1. Nobody; each; us; it

2. Some; his

3. You; she

4. All; we

5. none

6. Those

7. Themselves; they

8. Whoever; he; his

9. itself

10. Whatever; they; their; they; it

1.3 Verbs

1. are cleaned; converted

2. fail; are; develop

3. was; was held

4. went; had

5. will be

6. believed; were; was angered

7. gives; suggests; sit

8. was; could read

9. enjoy; would have required

10. Did; follow; did; find

1.4 Adjectives

1. The; puzzled; the; faded; the; royal

2. the; the; fifteen; the; small

3. the; famous; the; inaugural

4. Some; winter; small; propane; cold

5. Tremendous; young

6. Oceanographic; the; fragile; sea; the; coral

7. the; porch; our; expected

8. The; late; a; the

9. the; rusty; the; old; last; the; destructive

10. A; leaky; garbage; a; kitchen

1.5 Adverbs

1. weekly; now

2. seldom

3. slowly; purposefully

4. soon

5. cautiously; longer

6. westward

7. carefully; suddenly; easily

8. partially; late; quickly

9. quietly; in; gradually

10. forcefully; deliberately

1.6 Conjunctions, Prepositions, and Interjections

Conjunctions	Prepositions	Interjections
1. and	at	
2.	throughout of on	
3. and	in before	
4.	on of	
5. for	on	
6. if		well
7. but		
8.		no
9. so	in	
10. nor if		

1.7 Same Word; Several Functions

Individual responses will vary. The following are good possibilities.

1. like: preposition   Like his master, the dog is aggressive and fiercely loyal.

          adjective   On this and like celebrations, the children bring gifts for each other.

          verb   "Do you like the current best seller?" inquired the instructor.

2. water: noun   The water is clear and cold today.

          verb   I water the garden in hot weather.

          adjective   The water fountain has been broken for weeks.

3. well: noun   An uncovered well is very dangerous and is therefore illegal in most states.

          interjection   "Well," shouted the irate customer, "I shall speak to the manager!"

          adverb   The directions for the medication explicitly warned to shake well before using.

4. light: noun   Turn the light out.

          adjective   She wore a light coat to work.

          verb   We light the candles on the cake.

5. open: adjective   Old biplanes always had open cockpits.

          noun   Most political scandals eventually will be in the open.

          verb   The Air Force will open most bases to visitors on Veterans Day.

6. house: noun   The house on the corner is for sale.

        adjective   The house rent is due.

        verb   The case will house a collection of stamps.

7. total: noun   We have the total for the month's expenses.

        adjective   The total destruction from the fire was disheartening.

        verb   The clerk will total the bill.

8. paint: noun   The paint is still wet.

        adjective   The paint can is empty.

        verb   We will paint until this afternoon.

9. paper: noun   The paper is very thin.

        verb   We must paper the walls in our den.

        adjective   A paper banner decorated the new home.

10. down: noun   The down in the pillow is soft.

        verb   The Vikings downed the ball on the goal line.

        preposition   Bridge construction slowed traffic down the road.

2.1 The Parts of Sentences

Subject	Predicate	Predicate Adjective	Predicate Nominative	Direct Object	Indirect Object
1. solution	came				
2. water	cascaded				
3. contrast repetition	are		ingredients		
4. clouds	are		particles		
5. Brahms	wrote			sym- phonies	
6. arrangement	contained			pro- fusion	
7. ships	are being discovered				
8. pilots	put slip			planes	
9. headlines	reported			arrival	
10. blackberry it	is is used	edible			

2.2   The Parts of Sentences

	Subject	Predicate	Predicate Adjective	Predicate Nominative	Direct Object	Indirect Object
1.	grand-parents	regale				grand-children
2.	plans	are com-pleted				
3.	forger	can paint			copies	
4.	Franz Liszt	was	instrumental			
5.	Latin America	was settled				
6.	Arthur Wynne	devised			puzzle	
7.	Inter-national Balloon Fiesta	takes			place	
8.	use	is				
9.	Salaries	are	highest			
10.	One	notices			differences	

2.3 Phrases

1. modifier of <u>error</u>

2. modifier of <u>raced</u>

3. noun as subject of sentence

4. noun as subject of sentence

5. predicate nominative

6. modifier of <u>sweep</u>

7. modifier of <u>construction</u>

8. modifier of <u>billboards</u>

9. verb as predicate

10. noun as subject of sentence

2.4 Phrases

Individual responses will vary. The following are good possibilities.

1. Many travelers, concerned about increasing airline fares, have begun taking charter flights.

2. He wanted to hear the concert at eight o'clock.

3. He wanted to help by giving some of his time to the project.

4. Melissa walked through the entrance to the science exhibition.

5. The cake disappeared from the kitchen counter when the children came home.

6. Many old homes throughout the state have been restored to their original beauty.

7. The woman feared she was complicating the instructions by using too many technical words.

8. The man told everything except the truth to get out of trouble.

9. The soldiers were led into battle by a courageous officer.

10. A few lamps will illuminate the rooms.

11. We were now in the rapids, coursing down the river.

12. The single refuge the family could find was a cabin.

13. Our grandmother has treasured the memory of the trip.

14. After changing our plans, we had a good vacation.

15. The instructor decided to divide the class.

16. Elaine always can be trusted to say what is right.

17. Below the surface of the ocean, the pilot noticed a shadow that might be a sunken galleon.

18. The light brown coat had been discarded by someone.

19. The two students never had participated in a debate.

20. Our team suffered a humiliating defeat.

2.5 Verbals and Verbal Phrases

1. Carrying her wet shoes (participle; adjective; modifies salesperson)

2. To annoy his opponent (infinitive; adverb; modifies tapped)

3. to move closer to the front of the auditorium (infinitive; noun; direct object)

4. Constructed in 1885 (participle; adjective; modifies house)

5. to find links between left-handedness and a number of diseases (infinitive; adverb; modifies able)

6. Trained to hunt small burrowing animals (participle; adjective; modifies dachshund)

7. Walking to work (gerund; noun; subject)

8. Tempted by the smell of fresh bread (participle; adjective; modifies she)

9. to gather as much information as they can (infinitive; noun; direct object)

10. Swinging back and forth in the soft summer night (participle; adjective; modifies lantern)

11. to move his library into the garage (infinitive; noun; direct object)

12. to scatter when the owner walks in (infinitive; noun; direct object)

13. Using ultrasonic techniques (participle; adjective; modifies doctors)

14. to foster an awareness of our cultural inheritance (infinitive; noun; predicate nominative)

15. weaving colorful ponchos (gerund; noun; object of preposition)

16. draining of marshes (gerund; noun; direct object)

17. learning how emotions influence behavior (gerund; noun; predicate nominative)

18. working under strenuous conditions in the Arctic (participle; adjective; modifies Archeologists)

19. To enjoy television (infinitive; adverb; modifies needs)

20. to be selected for awards (infinitive; adjective; modifies employees)

2.6 Clauses

1. noun

2. adverb

3. adjective

4. adverb

5. adverb

6. adjective

7. adjective

8. noun

9. adverb

10. adverb

11. noun

12. adjective

13. adverb

14. noun

15. adverb

16. adverb

17. noun

18. adjective

19. adverb

20. noun

2.7 Clauses

Individual responses will vary. The following are good possibilities.

1. When glass telephone lines were developed, more calls could be carried on a single line than on conventional copper wires.

2. We could not arrange for flight reservations for this weekend, so we will have to wait until later to start our vacation.

3. The realtor was enthusiastic about the home, yet we decided the price was too high.

4. Sam wanted to know where the information desk in the hotel was located.

5. The dinner tasted terrible; moreover, it was extremely expensive.

6. The temperature began to drop and snow began to fall; nevertheless, we continued to ski until almost dark.

7. Whichever choice we make, we may find problems.

8. If we do not receive a refund for the faulty blender we bought, we will shop more carefully next time.

9. As they played, we talked.

10. Unless we work swiftly, we may not have time to see an early movie.

2.8 Kinds of Sentences

1. s

2. s

3. cd

4. s

5. s

6. s

7. s

8. cx

9. s

10. cd

3.1 Sentence Fragments

1. fragment
   fragment

2. fragment
   sentence

3. fragment
   fragment

4. sentence
   fragment

5. sentence
   sentence

6. fragment
   sentence

7. fragment
   sentence

8. sentence
   sentence

9. fragment
   fragment

10. fragment
    sentence

3.2   Sentence Fragments

1.   Prairie dogs greet each other in a strange way, by kissing.

2.   Knights wore capes over their armor because their crests
     indicated that they would be valuable as hostages held for
     ransom.

3.   The bottom of the ocean may be a dangerous place to dump
     nuclear waste, for scientists have detected the existence of
     violent storms on the ocean floor.

4.   Concerned that the prices might be raised, people often buy
     new appliances.

5.   Posted on the wall, the deteriorating circus advertisement was
     moved by a slight breeze.

6.   Stretching the entire length of the continent, the Andes
     Mountains dominate the geography of western South America.

7.   Once limited to the Western states, rodeos now enjoy national
     popularity.

8.   Gazing out across the horizon, the solitary woman did not see
     the sea gulls wading on the beach.

9.   Although the Star Wars films have been immensely popular, they
     have yet to attract the number of fans that still enjoy the
     Star Trek television series.

10. Country-western music is now more popular than any other
     musical style, even more popular than the rock music that
     began in the 1950s.

3.3 Comma Splices; Fused Sentences

Methods of correction will vary.

1. comma splice

2. fused sentence

3. fused sentence

4. fused sentence

5. comma splice

6. fused sentence

7. comma splice

8. fused sentence

9. comma splice

10. fused sentence

3.4 Comma Splices; Fused Sentences

Methods of correction will vary.

1. fused sentence

2. comma splice

3. fused sentence

4. fused sentence

5. fused sentence

6. fused sentence

7. comma splice

8. fused sentence

9. comma splice

10. fused sentence

4.1 Verb Forms

1. lay

2. hung

3. taken

4. borne

5. shown

6. sit

7. lain

8. lay

9. sit

10. raise

4.2 Verb Forms

1. froze

2. rang

3. broke

4. raged

5. slept

6. began

7. stolen

8. slid

9. lay

10. bursting

4.3 Verb Forms

1. risen
2. lying
3. written
4. seemed
5. ridden
6. bear
7. came
8. sank
9. Rung
10. paid

4.4 Tenses and Sequence of Tenses

1. passed

2. comes

3. have asked

4. to be replaced

5. returned

6. to have

7. has been lowered

8. clean; create

9. have linked

10. played

4.5 Voice

1. The county commissioners devised a new budget formula.

2. The thirsty spectators drank hundreds of cases of soft drinks.

3. The state engineers inspected the old bridge.

4. A few fans who still remembered him greeted the aging actor.

5. The directors made last-minute changes on the movie set.

6. Chuck-wagon cooks on cattle drives, who rarely had time to construct ovens, invented both hoecake and hardtack.

7. Visitors commonly sight flying squirrels in the vast interior of the Okefenokee Swamp.

8. The air controller cleared Flight 481 for take-off despite the heavy fog.

9. Musicologists have traced the roots of some American music to British, Scottish, Welsh, and Irish folk songs.

10. Thousands of Europeans now buy fashions created by American designers.

5.1 Subject and Verb Agreement

	Subject	Verb
1.	defect	is
2.	conversation	enlivens
3.	visiting; driving	are
4.	reports; debates	convince
5.	time	comes
6.	crowd	was
7.	who	lives
8.	speaker	was
9.	We	were
10.	Americans	are

5.2 Subject and Verb Agreement

	Subject	Verb
1.	policies	have been
2.	workshop	was
3.	majority	are
4.	vegetables; flowers	grow
5.	Whoever	says
6.	Science Club	participates
7.	Mary Ashley; Sonja Taylor; Ruthie Johns	were
8.	mural	was
9.	desire	sells
10.	lack	causes

6.1 Pronouns: Agreement and Reference

1. they

2. they

3. it

4. who

5. themselves

6. its

7. their

8. their lives

9. which

10. it

6.2 Pronouns: Agreement and Reference

1. their

2. it requires

3. its

4. they

5. who

6. their

7. their

8. they are

9. it

10. their

6.3 Case

1. who

2. I

3. them

4. their

5. who

6. us

7. he

8. themselves

9. her

10. whoever

6.4   Case

1. whom

2. we

3. me

4. I

5. my

6. Whom

7. we

8. they

9. me

10. Whoever

6.5 Case

1. We

2. I

3. whoever

4. me

5. we

6. his

7. I

8. who

9. who

10. us

7.1 Adjective or Adverb?

1. well

2. closely

3. viciously

4. quickly

5. warmly

6. good

7. well

8. frequently

9. vast

10. Really

11. close

12. quickly

13. well

14. largest; larger; more

15. abundant; stricter

16. possible

17. best

18. rapidly; accurately

19. solidly; strongly

20. usually

7.2 Adjective or Adverb?

1. cautiously

2. smallest

3. Normally

4. careful

5. heavily

6. quickly (preferred form; some dictionaries give both)

7. really; clearly

8. glum; worse

9. carefully

10. careful

8.1 Excessive Coordination

Individual responses will vary. The following are good possibilities.

1. The production line moved slowly because there were many breakdowns, and the employees were annoyed.

2. Preparing to finish the facial features, the portrait artist carefully mixed the pigments as his subject sat patiently.

3. When our retirement check arrived today, we deposited it and began our vacation.

4. Today is the last day of the year, and the store begins taking inventory on Monday, hoping to finish by Friday.

5. As the water cascaded over the falls, we watched the salmon leaping into the air and wondered what compelled them to such struggle.

6. Old-fashioned, frightening fairy tales taught safety. When children heard them, they were likely to stay on the path in the woods or near home.

7. Developed during World War II, the bazooka was an antitank weapon named after an odd musical instrument created by a popular comedian of the 1940s.

8. Discovered in the eighteenth century, sun spots have remained a mystery, but now scientists are beginning to understand these solar phenomena.

9. Parents who refuse to listen to their children and thus to encourage their talking may inhibit their verbal expression of fear and hostility.

10. Recently discovered in a remote area of the Philippines, the Tasaday are living examples of Stone Age people.

8.2 Subordination

1. A

2. B

3. B

4. B

5. B

6. B

7. B

8. B

9. B

10. B

8.3 Subordination

Individual responses will vary. The following are good possibilities.

1. While many television stations in the United States are on the air twenty-four hours a day, many foreign countries carefully regulate the number of broadcasting hours.

2. According to many experts, economic improvement continues in the United States because corporate management has improved.

3. Because the incidents of industrial theft are increasing, many companies are installing elaborate security systems.

4. Because radio was a very popular form of entertainment in the 1930s and 1940s, many people thought television would only be useful for educational and public-information programs.

5. When the large, beautiful murals were painted in the entrance, many people found them especially appealing.

6. Because Elaine was an industrious employee and was studying accounting at a local college, she was soon to be promoted to a position in management.

7. Because many people did not understand the meaning of such terms as "head of household" and "parochial" on the 1970 census form, the 1980 census form contained many simpler terms.

8. When Americans take their vacations in the early spring, they avoid the heavy winter rains and the dry summer months.

9. Flamingoes, which wade in search of food, are large birds with red or pink plumage, long legs and necks, and bills that turn downward at the tip.

10. The justice of the peace, the lowest-level magistrate in a state court system, performs marriages, administers oaths, and considers minor offenses that otherwise would crowd the dockets of higher courts.

8.4 Completeness and Comparisons

Individual responses will vary. The following are good possibilities.

1. Brad was happier this year than he was last year.

2. Modern jetliners are different from the jetliners of a few years ago.

3. The aircraft flying over the neighborhood have annoyed and continue to annoy residents.

4. Joyce thinks her new pickup truck is better than Trent's.

5. The new draperies cost me more than my mother's draperies cost.

6. Forgetting a school assignment is worse than any other mistake in school.

7. The tenant in the apartment was both interested in and suspicious of his neighbors.

8. The new investigative reporter was as good as some of the older reporters, if not better.

9. The new play at our local theater is one of the most interesting this season, if not the most.

10. My date likes me better than my friend Jane likes me.

8.5 Completeness and Comparisons

Individual responses will vary. The following are good possibilities.

1. In many cases laser surgery is more efficient than conventional surgery.

2. The library staff worked harder this year than ever before.

3. Many children understand their personal problems better than their parents do.

4. A completely rebuilt engine is usually just as dependable as a new engine.

5. My stereo equipment produces better sound than Tom's.

6. The lawyer was both involved with and concerned about the trial's outcome.

7. For children simple building blocks are as enjoyable as more expensive toys, if not more enjoyable.

8. The new business regulations are both examples of and guides to the administration's traditional economic policies.

9. The clerk had never been and never would be eligible for a long vacation because he took so many days off during the year.

10. Sri Lanka, formerly Ceylon, has been and continues to be the world's chief supplier of natural cinnamon.

8.6 Consistency

Individual responses will vary. The following are good possibilities.

1. I enjoy a cold glass of iced tea because I feel refreshed after I drink it.

2. Each of you has been given complete instructions, so you should not make any mistake.

3. We thought the light at the end of the tunnel was a sign of hope, but it was just a train coming in our direction.

4. Dreams are not necessarily accidental, for they often are considered efforts of the subconscious to work out real problems.

5. The article in the newspaper is very critical of the congressman and will be very damaging if he chooses to run again.

6. The cheetah is very tired after chasing its quarry and usually rests for several minutes before it eats.

7. The woman discovered the real identity of her friend after she had known (knew) her for twenty years.

8. After we had been hiking for several days, we grew tired and stopped to rest.

9. One of my closest friends is Larry Marconi, who is my neighbor.

10. The dam will hold huge amounts of water and will provide irrigation for the hundreds of farms in the nearby valley.

9.1 Position of Modifiers

Individual responses will vary. The following are good possibilities.

1. Quickly going up the stairs tired her.

2. With skill and patience, most fishermen catch fish.

3. The contract with the added clauses was signed today.

4. With great skill stuntmen crash cars into walls.

5. The community voted recently to turn a wooded area into a city park.

6. Suddenly reaching an arm through the bars of the cage, the monkey tore the man's pocket.

7. Effortlessly the motorcyclist turned sharply right and missed the barrier on the race track.

8. At the crossing the train pulling fifty boxcars and a caboose passed the auto.

9. Walking across the new sidewalk, pedestrians stepped in the cement.

10. Proudly showing off their new uniforms, the band marched down the street.

9.2   Position of Modifiers

Individual responses will vary. The following are good possibilities.

1. Reaching into the canoe, I dropped the camera into the swift
    current.

2. The engineer brought the experimental equipment, before being
    tested, to the laboratory.

3. From the ridge I saw an eagle soaring through the air.

4. Visiting the South Carolina and Georgia coasts, people can
    hear Americans who speak Gullah, an English-African dialect.

5. The judge's crowded days were made easier when he hired two
    additional secretaries.

6. Receiving a substantial raise, the worker could repair his
    house.

7. Using the office's newest electric typewriter, the secretary
    typed the letter.

8. When the wind died, the rain soon came.

9. Frequently television stations that run too many old movies
    lose viewers.

10. One who uses profanity often hurts oneself rather than others.

9.3 Separation of Elements

Individual responses will vary. The following are good possibilities.

1. If you have the opportunity, visit us soon.

2. At best, we knew that our taxes would increase slightly next year.

3. After the debris was cleared by the Army Corps of Engineers, the stream dropped below flood stage.

4. We wanted easily to avoid traffic.

5. After finishing their late afternoon shopping, people often have to drive home in heavy traffic.

6. Whenever people plan a trip, they always need to make certain the police are notified that they will be away from home.

7. Although it is sometimes a great mistake, eating in new restaurants is usually quite exciting.

8. Using the money she had earned as a clinical psychologist, Maria bought the stereo equipment she had wanted for several years.

9. Through the living room window, Micah watched with envy as his older brother and sister left for the first day of school.

10. Although she had not received any information, there was hope that Nichole would hear about her scholarship in a few days.

9.4 Parallelism

Individual responses will vary. The following are good possibilities.

1. The man was neither for new taxes nor against them.

2. The class went to the library for a lecture, for a tour, and for work on research papers.

3. The driver raced into town and drove to the center of the business district.

4. The new office building is tall, spacious, and landscaped.

5. The family intended to drive to the park, unpack the lunch, and walk to the game.

6. Travelers crossing southern Texas pass through Beaumont, Houston, San Antonio, and El Paso.

7. The attorney advised her client to testify in his own behalf and not to take the Fifth Amendment.

8. At school he found that he hated eating in the cafeteria, studying for his chemistry class, and doing his laundry.

9. After shopping at the department store, the two friends visited an art gallery and then watched a movie.

10. Although the fire inside the cabin was warm, the air was damp, the walls were cold, and the wind whispered through the cracks near the windows.

9.5 Parallelism

Individual responses will vary. The following are some good possibilities.

1. The weather reporter predicted rain and said that it would not last all day.

2. The timid soul was afraid of dogs and terrified of cats.

3. The singer's voice was magnificent, and the crowd applauded her.

4. Either one studies now, or one fails later.

5. Camping is great fun if one is not bothered by the bites of fleas, ticks, and mosquitoes.

6. To renew one's spirit, to test one's endurance, and to feel at peace with nature--these are the benefits of survival hikes.

7. Our vacation will be a success if we visit Carlsbad Caverns, the White Sands National Park, and Yellowstone Park.

8. The contractor opposed the scientists' request that he delay construction and let them excavate the archeological site.

9. The Treasury Department scrutinized all the amendments to the tax bills for unintentional loopholes, typographical errors, and windfall tax credits for special interests.

10. Pine trees are the most profitable investment for the forest-products industry; they grow fast, they provide lumber as well as pulp, and they provide naval stores such as turpentines and resins.

9.6 Variety in Sentences

Individual responses will vary. The following are some good possibilities.

1. Chicago's <u>World's Columbian Exhibition</u> began in 1893 and included over 686 acres lighted by electricity and the first Ferris wheel, the invention of George Washington Ferris.

2. The Roaring Twenties that followed World War I produced a group called flaming youth, perhaps the first young people to take themselves seriously as separate and distinct.

3. George Pullman built the first dining car in 1868, naming it the <u>Delmonico</u> after a famous New York City family of restaurateurs.

4. The company wants to promote its new product; hence it begins its sales campaign this week to feature its new line of furniture.

5. Clothing made of synthetic materials has been popular since World War II, but cotton is becoming popular again because it can now be made into a fabric that will hold a permanent press.

6. Termites do considerable damage, and homeowners may suspect their presence when they see large red ants, called carpenter ants, which eat termites.

7. Shortly after 9:00 P.M., the lights flickered briefly and went out a few minutes later.

8. The costs of owning a swimming pool are greater than the initial construction expenses; pools must be routinely maintained, and additional liability insurance must be procured by the swimming-pool owner.

9. Soft contact lenses are quite popular but require more care than hard contact lenses, for they must be washed daily and cleaned monthly with a special solution.

10. Although Norsemen are credited with discovering the New World around 1000 A.D. and Columbus is supposed to have discovered America in the fifteenth century, the first people to find the New World probably crossed a land bridge between Siberia and Alaska between 18,000 and 14,000 B.C.

9.7 Variety in Sentences

Individual responses will vary. The following are some good possibilities.

1. Six years after she started competition in the city tournaments, she won the women's amateur tennis championship.

2. An old car is uncomfortable, uses too much oil, and frequently fails to start.

3. The runner beat his opponents in the meet, broke his best time, and set a world record.

4. The earthquake interrupted communications, damaged several highways, and destroyed an entire section of the city.

5. The famous novelist finished his twentieth book last summer, toured several countries, and won the Nobel Prize.

6. When fog began to cover the Golden Gate Bridge, drivers turned on their headlights, slowed their cars, and prepared themselves for delays.

7. After the machinist lost her position, she searched the help-wanted advertisements for a new job, wrote letters listing her qualifications, and was interviewed by several companies.

8. Both political candidates have previous public service; they have served on the local school board, on the state board of mines, and in the United States Senate.

9. After the dam collapsed, the river rapidly reached flood level.

10. Because the weather reports predicted icy conditions above 2000 feet, we decided not to fly our small plane to Atlanta.

9.8 Variety in Sentences

1. periodic

2. loose

3. periodic

4. loose

5. loose

6. loose

7. loose

8. periodic

9. loose

10. periodic

9.9 Variety in Sentences

Individual responses will vary. The following are some good possibilities.

1. When I went to college, learning to live in the dormitory was difficult for me.

2. Although the days were often colder than we had expected, we toured Nova Scotia in August.

3. If you want to avoid making careless errors, you must follow the directions carefully.

4. In east-central Montana, I hiked to Big Dry Creek and Little Dry Creek.

5. When the bowl finally came to me, there were no mashed potatoes left.

6. Though many people prefer to call it the Coyote State, South Dakota is nicknamed the Sunshine State.

7. Though they do not receive as much money as other sports figures receive, rodeo champions earn large sums of money each year.

8. When you are finished, you will have to clean up the mess.

9. Because it is very rare, a 1928 Graf Zeppelin stamp is desired by every collector.

10. On the morning before the contract expired, the building was finished.

10.1   The Comma with Independent Clauses

1.   , and   About one-third of the passengers on the <u>Mayflower</u>
              left England for religious reasons, and the other
              two-thirds were adventurers.

2.   , but   The nuclear power industry claims that atomic plants
              have been criticized unfairly, but many scientists
              believe that the problems are even greater than
              originally thought.

3.   C

4.   , and   The Labrador retriever sat in the back of the pickup
              truck, and it seemed to enjoy the wind blowing in its
              face.

5.   C

6.   C

7.   C

8.   C

9.   , but   The diver realized the danger in attempting a new
              record height in the brisk wind, but he asked the
              judges for permission to raise the platform.

10. , and   Many restaurants in New England are famous for their
              seafood, and some also have fine views of the
              Atlantic Ocean and the fishing boats that sail along
              the coast.

10.2   The Comma with Independent Clauses

1. , and   There were no rooms available at the resort, and we
             had to return home.

2. , but   Vacationing in Hawaii is exciting, but traveling
             closer to home is less expensive.

3. , so   Many students seek part-time employment during their
             vacations, so unemployment rates rise during the
             summer months.

4. , but   Patience, persistence, and determination are all
             necessary to train a dog, but the most important
             requirement is consistency.

5. , and   Many of the books in the library were very old, and
             the librarian knew there was little money available
             to save them.

6. , but   The docks were empty when the ship began to approach,
             but suddenly they came alive with workers ready to
             unload the cargo.

7. , but   The small painting being auctioned was by a rela-
             tively minor sixteenth-century artist, but it was
             valued at almost a quarter of a million dollars.

8. C

9. C

10. , and   Infra-red photographs of the earth's geography help
             scientists to determine the extent of droughts, and
             they also are invaluable aids in the search for
             mineral deposits.

10.3   The Comma with Items in Series

1. . . . oil, natural gas, and electricity . . . .

2. . . . words, adds new ones, and develops . . . .

3. . . . flashed, the stereo played loudly, and the
    revelers . . . .

4. . . . refrigerators, ranges, and sinks.

5. . . . the javelin throw, the broad jump, and the mile run.

6. . . . mowing, hauling, and cultivating.

7. . . . itemized deductions, computed our refund, and now
    must . . . .

8. . . . it had bitten the mail carrier, run our neighbor's cat
    up a tree, and chased a delivery truck.

9. . . . eat harmful insects, scatter seeds, and spread
    pollen . . . .

10. . . . watched several cartoons, a serial, and two movies . . .

10.4 The Comma with Coordinate Adjectives

1. quiet, desultory

2. bright, cheerful greeting

3. quick, intelligent answers

4. short, rude

5. long, hard hours

6. new, well-designed by-pass

7. sturdy, inexpensive trampolines

8. modern, energy-efficient ways

9. agile, deft movements

10. best, least expensive medicine

10.5 The Comma After Introductory Clauses or Phrases

1. C

2. orchestra,   Although Michael liked playing in the orchestra, he did not like practicing.

3. be,   Whatever the problem might be, Jerry was usually responsible for it.

4. lines,   Because the storm had torn down the power lines, the family had to spend the night in a motel.

5. sized,   After Linda's engagement ring had been sized, she showed it to her friends.

6. C

7. player,   Although I was a good football player, my brother was better than I.

8. C

9. sets,   Although citizens-band radios are not as power-ful as short-wave sets, they nevertheless furnish hours of enjoyment to many motorists.

10. C

10.6 The Comma After Introductory Clauses or Phrases

1. C; or
   optional
       After the demise of vaudeville, many of its stars became radio and television entertainers.

2. C

3. success,
       Even though the meeting was considered a success, many in the group felt much of the work remained unfinished.

4. C; or
   optional

5. limousine,
       Stepping into her limousine, the diplomat suddenly turned and waved to the crowd.

6. maps,
       After examining their road maps, travelers still may fail to turn onto the right road.

7. it,
       Because doctors, parents, and students are requesting it, physical hygiene is being taught in many public schools.

8. vapor,
       Although most of Mars' visible water now appears as polar ice and atmospheric vapor, water may have flowed in rivers on the Martian surface thousands of years ago.

9. C; or
   optional
       To escape the crowd, some people leave a few minutes before shops close.

10. C

10.7 The Comma with Nonrestrictive Elements

1. C

2. Pier fishing, which is especially popular in this area, will remain unregulated.

3. C

4. C

5. Dr. Pamela M. Smith, who is the Vice President for Continuing Education, delivered the commencement address.

6. C

7. Blueberries, which may be cultivated in large orchards, make splendid jellies and jams.

8. The new municipal airport, which opened last week, is several miles from the city.

9. Professional counseling in elementary school, which is a relatively new field, can make a dramatic difference in the scholastic performance of many young children.

10. John Richardson, who is the chef at my father's restaurant, does not like to prepare food for large groups.

10.8 The Comma--All Uses

1. On July 1, 1981, we will begin a new training program for our older employees.

2. Alicia McMurray, C.P.A., was employed by the firm of Feldman, Parsons, and Ames.

3. We wrote a letter to our congressman's regional office in Richmond, Virginia, to complain about his recent stand on taxes.

4. "In conclusion," said the long-winded, dull speaker, "I would like to thank all of you for coming--men, women, boys, girls-- all of you."

5. The international Morse code, a form of the original Morse code used in international telegraphy, is sometimes called the continental code.

6. Whenever we hear that snow has fallen in the nearby mountains, we pack up the car and spend the weekend there.

7. The American Council for Learned Societies, located at 345 East 46th Street, New York, New York 10017, sponsors many kinds of fellowships in various academic disciplines.

8. On this date, October 12, 1984, the small collection of houses called Arno, New Mexico, was formally incorporated, and it installed its first mayor, city council, and school board.

9. "Although it is a relatively small city, Bismarck, North Dakota, is the state capital and is twice as large as Pierre, South Dakota, which is also a state capital," stated the visiting lecturer in Geography 101.

10. Sandra O'Connor, a jurist from Arizona, is the first woman appointed to the United States Supreme Court.

10.9 The Comma--All Uses

1. The woman in charge of personnel, Margaret Childes, requires
    a psychological profile of each new employee.

2. Any citizen of the United States may communicate with the
    President simply by addressing a letter to 1600 Pennsylvania
    Avenue, Washington, D.C.

3. Although pumice is quite porous and even appears to be spongy,
    it is a form of volcanic rock used as an abrasive.

4. "The Book Exchange," the notice read, "will be open on Monday,
    December 19."

5. To settle legal disputes among themselves, many nations turn
    to the International Court of Justice, the main judicial body
    of the United Nations.

6. C

7. The eager, industrious volunteers worked to complete the home-
    coming float.

8. Lifting the antique glass to the light to examine its color,
    examining the engraving, and lightly tapping its sides, the
    expert judged it to be quite valuable.

9. To a shaggy, long-haired dog that can find little relief from
    the summer heat, a cool, bare concrete floor is a great
    blessing.

10. On January 18, 1985, Charles Richardson, an active man through-
    out his life, will celebrate his eighty-seventh birthday.

10.10 Unnecessary Commas

1. The mountains near our home are noted for the beautiful, clear lakes and the many types of birds and plants.

2. The ferocious black hornet is really a member of the wasp family and is, believe it or not, a very social insect.

3. The dingo, a wolf-like, wild dog of Australia, is a natural enemy of sheep herds.

4. In The Red Badge of Courage, (optional) Stephen Crane brings to life the psychological conflicts of young Henry Fleming, the hero.

5. An unusually large black bat quickly flew from room to room in the caverns several hundred feet underground.

6. Of some botanical interest is a plant called rattlesnake root, which has tubers that supposedly cure rattlesnake bites--at least many early settlers thought so.

7. The famous Oregon Trail covered two thousand miles of frontier from Independence, Missouri, to Portland, Oregon, and was heavily traveled during the westward migrations of the nineteenth century.

8. The unusually careful driver ahead of us slowed everyone in our lane.

9. One of the shells that we found at the beach turned out to be valuable.

10. The last of the South American artifacts shown at the museum were packed and prepared for shipping at the end of the week.

10.11 Unnecessary Commas

1. "A gentleman, sir," he quoted, "kneels only to pray or propose. Furthermore, a gentleman removes his tie only for sleeping."

2. When invited to an informal cookout, she appears in fashionable attire of fiery red and orange silk; and her husband always wears a baggy, wrinkled brown suit.

3. Of all the poems I have read recently, Thomas Hardy's lyric "The Darkling Thrush" and Alfred, Lord Tennyson's In Memoriam seem the most pertinent to our times.

4. The shadow of the massive, ageless oak fell upon the young and carefree lovers as they planned with infinite faith for the future.

5. So great was the influence of Thomas Paine on his own time that John Adams suggested that the era be called "The Age of Paine."

6. One should never be ashamed, however, of being somewhat sentimental, for a certain amount of sentimentality can help keep a person warm and human.

7. By 1910, (optional) some demographers predicted that the population of Western Europe would begin to decline and that, (optional) by the end of the century, (optional) Eastern Europe would be more populous than Western Europe.

8. Efficient construction workers at the building site completed the foundation in less than a week.

9. Our new piano will be delivered this week, possibly by Wednesday.

10. The Coast Guard launch skipped across the water, quickly slowed, and then turned toward the pier.

11.1   The Semicolon

1. In 1900 the average life expectancy for an American was 47.3 years; in 1975 this average had increased to 72.4 years.

2. Some railroads use simulated locomotives to train engineers; others depend on the traditional apprenticeship system.

3. An increase of dust particles in the earth's atmosphere may cause a general climatic cooling trend; they reflect sunlight and reduce solar heat.

4. Australia's Bicentennial gift to the United States was an endowed chair in Australian studies at Harvard University; another gift is a copy of Magna Charta from Great Britain.

5. Large banks may allow small, efficient data-processing firms to compute some of their paperwork; for example, payroll processing and stock transfers are often the work of con- tracted accounting firms.

6. Scientific prediction of earthquakes remains primitive and haphazard; nevertheless, scientists can make general predic- tions after monitoring magnetic changes along major faults.

7. Automatic transmissions and air conditioning account for higher automotive fuel costs: for a luxury, eight-cylinder car the additional cost per ten thousand miles may reach $350; for a compact car, $250; and for a six-cylinder subcompact, $200.

8. Scientists say that brain research offers the promise of treating many serious diseases; others claim that scientists may be exploring areas best left untouched.

9. The work was painfully slow; he didn't know whether he should weep or laugh.

10. For years aircraft designers have attempted to reduce the weight of planes by using lighter metals; now they are using reinforced lightweight materials that virtually eliminate most of the metal formerly used.

11.2   The Semicolon

1. The city manager proposed a graduated income tax; the city council preferred a citywide sales tax to increase revenues.

2. To the early Mormon settlers, the Colorado Plateau was unattractive; to later pioneers, it was a pastoral vista of tranquility and color.

3. Vinyl, which resembles leather, is a popular covering for contemporary-style sofas; cotton velvet, which resembles suede, is almost as popular.

4. Epoxy glue can join together almost any kind of material, except rubber and some plastics; indeed, the bond from the glue is often stronger than the original material.

5. Prospective pet owners should investigate thoroughly what kinds of animals best fit their lifestyles; then the pets they choose may become pleasures rather than nuisances to them.

6. When purchasing an automobile battery, the consumer should compare various brands and sizes; standards of comparison may include a battery's cold-cranking power, reserve capacity, ampere-hour capacity, and total number of plates.

7. A good set of tools should include a socket wrench, with various sockets and adapters; screwdrivers, conventional and Phillips' head; a hacksaw; and a hammer.

8. The fact that caffeine is an effective insecticide is not generally known; however, once this information reaches the public, many companies may develop new caffeine-free products.

9. Some people's lives are driven by desperation; others' lives are guided by inspiration.

10. At present NASA is choosing the basic design of the first permanent United States space station; as early as the mid-1990s, the first sections of the orbiter may be in place.

1. The quarterback's play--a tight-end screen pass--surprised both the defense and the fans. (Commas could have been used rather than dashes.)

2. Many theaters find that an 8:15 curtain time means fewer late-comers than one at 8:00.

3. The cotton gin--invented by a man from Massachusetts on a visit to Georgia--helped to shape the economic destinies of both North and South. (Commas could have been used rather than dashes.)

4. A good bird watcher makes identifications using the following characteristics: voice, color, size, type of bill, markings, and range.

5. There is one quality that endears two-year-olds to those around them--their desire to imitate adults.

6. Ragweed, mesquite, pine--all produce common allergies.

7. The most common means of evaluation--the intelligence test--is no longer considered sufficient as the sole criterion for placement in special classes. (Commas could have been used rather than dashes.)

8. All of us--John, Mary, and I--wanted the opening on the debate team.

9. After the FAA completed its examination of the wreckage, it concluded that there could be only one reason for the crash--pilot error.

10. Halfway down the page the following admonition appeared in bold print: DO NOT WRITE BELOW THIS LINE.

11.4   Parentheses and Brackets

1. The administration of Franklin D. Roosevelt (1932–1945) was the longest of any president.

2. Saint Valentine's Day (February 14) is observed in honor of a Christian martyr.

3. Boise (which rhymes with "noisy") is the capital of Idaho; it was built on the Oregon Trail.

4. The agronomists considered soybeans as the crop of the future because (1) they have few natural enemies; (2) they are high in protein; and (3) they require relatively little expensive fertilizer.

5. Seventeen thousand new Flashback cars (the model had just been introduced) had to be recalled because of faulty brakes.

6. The expert on etiquette (she had written four books on the subject) concluded: "Good manners reveal it [good breeding] therefore, one should take it seriously."

7. Many physicians believe that most people would enjoy good health if they would (a) eat modestly, (b) exercise regularly, and (c) maintain an optimistic attitude.

8. Before going on vacation, people should (1) stop all deliveries, (2) ask a neighbor to watch their house, and (3) make certain that all doors are locked and all windows are securely closed.

9. Someone (we think it is Mike Erlich) has been circulating memos that are quite funny to the office staff.

10. "That was the year [1965]," he said, "that we planned to expand our market to include the West Coast."

12.1 Quotation Marks and End Punctuation

1. "My ring is gone!" cried the frantic woman.

2. "Well," the sergeant said, "you don't have my permission."

3. "Keep your bike in top condition for safe riding," said the instruction booklet.

4. "What sort of experience leads a young person to choose the life of a surgeon?" inquired the patient.

5. The social scientist summarized as follows: "Because young people generally have values in opposition to those of adult society, youth can be classified as a genuine subculture."

6. "An increase in radon in well water," said the science reporter, "may become a means for geologists to predict earthquakes."

7. "So many foreign visitors were anticipated by Greek officials that they made arrangements for several ships to provide accommodations for tourists without hotel reservations," explained the travel agent.

8. "Stop! You've tried my patience to the limit!"

9. The press corps asked exactly what the role of the President's science adviser would be.

10. "Did you know that some of the officers in the American Revolution came to this country from Poland specifically to help us win the war?" asked the history instructor.

    "Our town, Pulaski, Tennessee, is named for one of them," a student answered.

    "Correct. That was Count Pulaski," responded the teacher.

12.2   Quotation Marks and End Punctuation

1. The article discussed why boys and girls differ in behavior even before puberty.

2. "To freeze peaches," droned the television chef, "use citric acid to prevent the fruit from turning brown."

3. Although considered strange by his friends, Raymond was actually very shy.

4. "Why do I have to go to the dentist?" the child asked.

5. Who said, "The only place he'd be the life of the party is in a mortuary"?

6. "Quick!" the driver screamed to the passerby. "The light will change shortly."

7. "When my daughter completes her B.S.," continued the proud father, "she expects to begin work toward her M.S. and eventually to earn her Ph.D."

8. When the diner looked at the burned steak, he complained to the waiter, "I said 'well done,' not cremated."

   "You said, 'very well done,' sir," replied the waiter.

9. "None of the current methods of increasing the energy supply of America appears to be adequate," writes Wilson Clark in "It Takes Energy to Get Energy."

10. "Can you come by the house today?" Mary asked.

    "No, I haven't the time," Craig answered. "But I can come tomorrow."

    "Fine, I'll see you then."

13.1 Italics

1. <u>U.S.A.</u> Today

2. <u>Lorry</u>, <u>truck</u>

3. <u>l</u>'s; <u>g</u>'s; <u>k</u>'s

4. <u>Columbia</u>

5. <u>Spirit</u> <u>of</u> <u>St.</u> <u>Louis</u>

6. <u>Chariots</u> <u>of</u> <u>Fire</u>

7. U.S.S. <u>New</u> <u>Jersey</u>

8. <u>Blue</u> <u>Highways</u>

9. <u>Fraggle</u> Rock

10. <u>fait</u> <u>accompli</u>

13.2 Italics

1. United States, Queen Elizabeth II

2. A Field Guide to the Birds

3. Science Digest

4. urbane, National Geographic, Discover

5. The Mouse Trap

6. roman à clef, Look Homeward, Angel

7. Ordinary People

8. Four Seasons

9. The Empire Strikes Back, Star Wars

10. Washington Post

14.1 Suffixes

1. compelling

2. devastating

3. notable

4. noticeable

5. reality

6. forbidden

7. writing

8. symptomatic

9. eatable

10. realistic

11. fullness (or fulness)

12. likable (or likeable)

13. subduing

14. interchangeable

15. massive

16. beauteous

17. committing

18. reversible

19. beginning

20. occurring

21. fried

22. frying

23. pluralistic

24. recurred

25. canceled (or cancelled)

14.2 Suffixes

1. denotation

2. believable

3. tardiness

4. possibility

5. compassionate

6. invalidate

7. truly

8. loneliness

9. conceivable

10. enviable

11. netting

12. directory

13. endured

14. prescribing

15. admittance

16. marvelous (or marvellous)

17. traveled (or travelled)

18. adequately

19. courageous

20. exploration

21. judgment (or judgement)

22. achievement

23. prettily

24. guaranteeing

25. proposal

14.3 Spelling with _ie_ and _ei_

1. conscience

2. relieve

3. conceit

4. mien

5. deign

6. pier

7. financier

8. sieve

9. deceit

10. either

11. series

12. relieve

13. view

14. friend

15. niece

16. foreign

17. feign

18. conceive

19. siege

20. neither

21. science

22. receipt

23. deceive

24. height

25. seize

14.4 Spelling with _ie_ and _ei_

1. forfeit

2. field

3. retrieve

4. piece

5. shriek

6. yield

7. achieve

8. deign

9. freight

10. heir

11. priest

12. conscientious

13. neighbor

14. reign

15. sleigh

16. omniscient

17. neigh

18. believe

19. perceive

20. weight

21. leisure

22. ceiling

23. milieu

24. pliers

25. Geiger

14.5 Plurals

1. elves

2. courtesies

3. trepidations

4. bastions

5. bureaucracies

6. cargoes (or cargos)

7. gypsies

8. thieves

9. antennae (or antennas)

10. oases

11. antitheses

12. bookshelves

13. heroes

14. committees

15. trauma (or traumata)

16. villages

17. essays

18. cemeteries

19. embargoes

20. locusts

21. halos (or haloes)

22. alumni

23. manifestoes (or manifestos)

24. media (or mediums)

25. criteria (or criterions)

14.6 Hyphenation

1. roadside

2. nowadays

3. seaside

4. eighty-five

5. letterhead

6. de-escalate

7. one hundred

8. transcontinental

9. nationwide

10. C

11. C

12. C

13. half-truth

14. percentage

15. C (or percent)

16. nonfiction

17. thing-in-itself

18. hubbub

19. semisolid

20. great-grandmother

21. pro-American

22. C

23. rewrite

24. ex-councilman

25. subterranean

14.7 Hyphenation and Syllabication

1. The cashier shortchanged the customer.

2. The garden club committee will meet Thursday morning.

3. A trouble-shooter came from the Maintenance Department.

4. We had a long discussion in class today over the usage of a word.

5. When I met Susan, I knew she was a born leader.

6. Physicians warn that quack remedies for arthritis--apple cider, vinegar, a dry climate, or a copper bracelet--have no medical value.

7. Bills designed to expand the active work force have been introduced in the House of Representatives.

8. Some political theorists believe that the Attorney General should be independent of the White House, and a congressional subcommittee is studying this suggestion.

9. The Department of Public Safety tries to discourage hitchhikers because many of them are victimized by so-called good-Samaritan drivers.

10. An increase of white-collar jobs, a decrease of blue-collar jobs, and an increase in the number of working wives will mean that 30 percent of all American families will earn $25,000 or more by 1990.

15.1 The Apostrophe

	Singular Possessive	Plural Possessive
1.	witness' or witness's	witnesses'
2.	wife's	wives'
3.	devotee's	devotees'
4.	Rivera's	Riveras'
5.	slogan's	slogans'
6.	Kent's	Kents'
7.	genius's	geniuses'
8.	Perez's	Perezes'
9.	druggist's	druggists'
10.	dictionary's	dictionaries'
11.	heroine's	heroines'
12.	cemetery's	cemeteries'
13.	poet's	poets'
14.	girl's	girls'
15.	fox's	foxes'
16.	church's	churches'
17.	Mathis' (or Mathis's)	Mathises'
18.	attorney's	attorneys'
19.	mother-in-law's	mothers-in-law's
20.	workman's	workmen's

21. specimen's   specimens'

22. Pakistani's   Pakistanis'

23. Westerner's   Westerners'

24. library's   libraries'

25. judge's   judges'

15.2   The Apostrophe

1. toys; plant's

2. physician's; prognosis

3. water's

4. Charles'; evenings

5. Waitresses'; its '78; city's

6. attorney's; o'clock; o'clock

7. father-in-law's; day's

8. 7's; E's

9. theirs; neighbor's

10. quarterback's; receiver's; defense's

15.3 Capitals

1. Trans; Building

2. Yukon; Bering Sea

3. Yule

4. educational television; children's programs

5. King; A; A; My

6. English; <u>young</u>; Swedish; English

7. stock companies

8. Prime Minister; Great; Second World War; art

9. public; essayist

10. Septuagint; Bible; Old Testament; legend; Jewish

15.4 Abbreviations and Numbers

1. We chose April 15 as an appropriate date to hear Representative Hasting's view on income tax.

2. Thirty-five percent of our stock was sold the first day the store opened.

3. When we retire in 1986, we plan to move to a small town just outside Denver, Colorado.

4. The Metropolitan Transit Authority purchased twenty-two new buses for $2,440,000.

5. Occupancy rates of hotels in some resort areas climbed as high as 90 percent during the Bicentennial celebration.

6. One lineman weighed 250 pounds; another, 240 pounds; the third, 260 pounds; and the last, 280 pounds--all for an average weight of 257.5 pounds.

7. The New York Times sent its best reporters to Washington, D.C., to cover the White House, Senate, and House of Representatives.

8. Most economists agree that countries with 50 percent inflation are in deep financial trouble.

9. On the twenty-fourth of December each year (or On December 24 each year) community choirs across the United States go caroling.

10. Reverend Smith, Senator Martinez, and Captain Briggs of the Air Force were present for the commissioning of the new lieutenants.

16.1 The Dictionary and Usage

1. besides

2. try to

3. number

4. well

5. criteria

6. compare to

7. every day

8. unique

9. implied

10. kind of

16.2 The Dictionary and Usage

1. fewer

2. as if

3. off

4. percentage

5. that

6. partially

7. sensuous

8. sometime

9. these kinds

10. farther

16.3 The Dictionary and Usage

1. all ready

2. where her father was

3. effect

4. agreed to

5. altogether

6. way

7. among

8. a while

9. bad

10. burst

16.4 The Dictionary and Usage

1. capitol

2. enthusiastic

3. all right

4. fewer

5. formalize

6. complemented

7. because

8. continuous

9. hanged

10. regardless

16.5 The Dictionary and Usage

1. <u>compared to</u>; compared with

2. <u>affects</u>, <u>less</u>; effects, fewer

3. <u>further</u>, <u>ways off</u>; farther, way

4. <u>reason . . . is because</u>, <u>those sort</u>; reason . . . is that, those sorts

5. <u>kind of a</u>; kind of

6. <u>all together</u>, <u>like</u>; altogether, as if

7. <u>affect</u>, <u>enthused</u>; effect, enthusiastic

8. <u>Fewer</u>, <u>besides</u>; less, beside

9. <u>bad</u>; badly

10. correct

16.6 The Dictionary and Usage

1. <u>compared . . . with</u>; compared to

2. <u>off of</u>; off

3. <u>kind of a</u>; kind of

4. <u>criteria</u>, <u>bust</u>; criterion, burst

5. <u>to try and</u>; to try to

6. <u>percent</u>, <u>everyday</u>; percentage, every day

7. <u>amount</u>, <u>already</u>; number, all ready

8. <u>reason . . . is because</u>; reason . . . is that

9. <u>bursted, between</u>; burst, among

10. <u>continually</u>; continuously

16.7   The Dictionary and Usage

One of the most exciting events of the nineteenth century was a

      unique
rather unique industrial world's fair held in the Crystal Palace in

                                  altogether
London, a glass building that looked all together fragile but was,

                            percentage
in fact, very strong. A large percent of the populace were so

enthusiastic
enthused about the display that some attended the show several

times. Inside the transparent building they were treated to

                                       hung
extensive displays of machinery and furniture; textiles were hanged

from the ceiling, and exotic plants were clustered in small groups

      way
all the ways down the central aisle. It was difficult for the

            try to   among
viewer to try and choose between the hundreds of exhibits, all so

                                         effect
plentiful and so highly decorated that they had a dazzling affect

on the eyes.

16.8 The Dictionary and Usage

                    number
A large <u>amount</u> of people would agree to the idea that going to the

circus was an exciting childhood event. The atmosphere itself had
                                                              sensuous
a special tang; even the sawdust hanging in the air was a <u>sensual</u>
                         a while
pleasure as if, for <u>awhile</u>, one could both smell and taste the

excitement. What a thrill it was when the lights went down and the
                                                    like
trapeze artist flew over the crowds <u>as</u> a bird on the wing, and how
                                                     burst
the audience jumped when the clown suddenly <u>bursted</u> a balloon
                                                 with
filled with water! Surely nothing can compare <u>to</u> the heart-stopping

experience of seeing the unprotected lion tamer taunting the king

of the beasts, who, snarling and growling, was ready to hurl him-
          off   Regardless
self <u>off of</u> the ledge in his cage. <u>Irregardless</u> of the time, the
                                              all ready
end always came too quickly; parents were <u>already</u> to leave while

children still sat starry-eyed, clutching the remains of sticky

candy apples or crumpled bags of popcorn.

16.9 The Dictionary and Standard English

Answers may vary with different dictionaries. Students should
compare and discuss their answers.

16.10 The Dictionary and Standard English

1. they're (they are)

2. mystery story

3. not sensible; foolish

4. silly; completely absurd

5. shirker

6. a small piece or lump; a sailor; a mouth

7. gentleman

8. man

9. enthusiastic

10. illustrates

11. pawn

12. nearly enough

13. discuss

14. would not have

15. succeed

16. sat around (sit around)

17. could have

18. regardless

19. given that

20. suspected

16.11 Improprieties

1. institutional

2. especially nice

3. goulash

4. educational experience

5. trivial incident

6. wooden mallet

7. wooden (or C)

8. frivolous

9. utopian

10. utility

11. unstable

12. unskilled

13. plundered

14. C

15. critical

16. C

17. C

18. handwritten

19. strummed

20. meandering

21. wandering

22. whiled

23. the new directive

24. cattle for slaughter

25. clinging

1. emulate

2. baleful

3. wasted

4. emollient

5. aid

6. obstinate

7. peer

8. alluded

9. abject

10. fete

11. delusion

12. its

13. waistline

14. their

15. feat

16. Altering

17. Passed

18. Proceeding

19. prescribe

20. psychic

21. sensory

22. morale

22. fiancée

24. grateful

25. conscience

16.13 Improprieties

1. reigned

2. moot

3. overt

4. leach

5. leeks

6. means

7. accrued

8. too

9. than

10. butted

11. plain

12. flaunt

13. material

14. kin

15. jibe

16. corporal

17. capitol

18. intuitive

19. loanwords

20. fare

21. site

22. Fore

23. poll

24. Council

25. flares

16.14 Idioms

1. the year 1922

2. Contrary to

3. Oblivious to

4. conducive to

5. indigenous to

6. bearing on

7. in the affirmative

8. die

9. cover to cover

10. dam

16.15 Idioms

1. fond of

2. joined

3. doted on

4. to turn down

5. insisted on

6. superior to

7. was uninteresting

8. reason is . . . that (not <u>because</u>)

9. In regard

10. C

16.16 Triteness

Individual responses will vary. The following are good possibilities.

1. He fought well but lost.

2. He was a friend as long as there was no trouble.

3. Jim was speeding until he was stopped by the police.

4. "You have bought during a declining market," said the doleful
    stockbroker to her disheartened client, "but do not give up."

5. San Francisco, a city that was rebuilt after suffering the
    effects of a devastating earthquake, exemplifies human courage
    and determination.

6. Old diaries, journals, and letters reveal that the early
    pioneers in the West found some of the wild country to be
    beautiful.

7. The chief targets of confidence men are gullible investors.

8. One is often reminded that virtue has intrinsic value.

9. The essence of most economists' complaints is that short-range
    political considerations take precedence over long-range
    economic policy.

10. The premise of international diplomacy is that words are
    preferable to war.

16.17 Triteness

Individual responses will vary. The following are good possibilities.

1. Famous authors are often considered to be extremely perceptive.

2. The United States traditionally has excelled in medical research.

3. Superior college athletes can bargain for lucrative contracts in professional sports.

4. The first British colonists in America quickly learned that charity and neighborliness were necessary for survival.

5. A few of these first colonists returned to England, but most endured.

6. Those willing to travel early in the morning usually spend less for airline fares.

7. We left quickly for our new home in Muleshoe, Texas.

8. The main duty of the public health officer is to prevent communicable diseases.

9. One could tell by his doleful face that Mary had hurt his feelings.

10. The batter hit the ball into the outfield, ran for first, then suddenly sped for second.

16.18 Wordiness

Individual responses will vary. The following are good possibilities.

1. William Harvey first wrote about the circulation of the blood.

2. His music pleased the audience.

3. Although Benjamin Franklin was not a great writer, he was a
    great man.

4. Americans have always applauded the tenacious underdog who
    tries to recover.

5. All human beings possess certain doctrines of natural rights.

6. Because of television the American's appreciation of the arts
    has obviously decreased.

7. There are many educational and social differences between high
    school and college.

8. Today a man hardly can be independent in education, economic
    theories, and personal philosophy.

9. Out our car window we saw the little cafe about which you had
    written.

10. A review of the evidence in your case justifies a new trial.

16.19 Wordiness

Individual responses will vary. The following are good possibilities.

1. Today we face enormously large economic problems.

2. We went to our school's library to gather material for our term papers.

3. The author's works contain many brief sentences that express basic truths.

4. Hunting big game with a camera is fully as dangerous as hunting big game with a rifle.

5. An ovenbird is an American warbler which builds on the floor of a forest a nest that resembles an oven.

6. Certain cities retain a small-town atmosphere in those neighborhoods characterized by unique ethnic charm.

7. For years the basic cultural foundation of this great nation was the small town with its small, homogeneous neighborhoods.

8. Beginning in the 1930s writers have often been interested in Hollywood as a setting for their novels.

9. Overflowing water from our bathroom stained the hall carpet.

10. The Doberman pinscher and the German shepherd, two breeds that are considered good guard dogs, may be compared in appearance, disposition, and physical prowess.

16.20 Wordiness

Individual responses will vary. The following are good possibilities.

1. Run-off elections draw fewer voters than regular elections.

2. We do not agree with the committee.

3. We shall conclude the evening's festivities with our school song.

4. Current research on the nervous system of the cockroach might lead to a cure for glaucoma, a disease of the eye.

5. Major political pollsters are worried about the trend of people refusing to answer questionnaires or to take part in interviews.

6. Some birdfeeders differ because birds have different eating habits and feeding requirements.

7. Mammoths, prehistoric beasts that looked like elephants, had hairy skin, shoulders as high as eleven feet, and tusks as long as thirteen feet.

8. Laws requiring motorcycle riders to wear crash helmets have saved many lives in the past and will do so in the future.

9. Our calendar is based on the Julian calendar, established by Julius Caesar, which fixed the length of the year at 365 days.

10. Our English teacher this term assigned books from a reading list.

16.21 Repetition

Individual responses will vary. The following are good possibilities.

1. Instant replays show that officials usually make correct calls and perform their duties responsibly.

2. After the bear market of the early 1970s, stockbrokers decided to diversify into securities other than common stocks.

3. The danger of dense cloud cover in heavily traveled air corridors is a midair collision.

4. Most populous cities are circumscribed by large beltways that prevent major traffic jams.

5. The situation comedy that is interesting, engaging, and prepossessing will always attract a television audience.

6. The respected judge of a debate never allows contempt or disparagement to be displayed on the debate floor.

7. Sewing one's own clothes is a way of saving money and allows one to choose a favorite style and fabric.

8. Successful football teams often have excellent kickers of field goals and extra points.

9. The good insurance adjustor must be constantly alert to evidence of impropriety while never forgetting to be fair.

10. Farmers' markets are enjoying a significant resurgence in larger cities; on good days, a farmer in New York, Seattle, Santa Fe, or Boston may gross a thousand dollars.

© 1986 Houghton Mifflin Company

16.22 Repetition

Individual responses will vary. The following are good possibilities.

1. Volcanoes erupt with terrific force, spewing hot, molten lava
    and scattering ash for miles.

2. Floods are ever-present dangers to the farmer.

3. Powdery snow on ski slopes must be monitored constantly for
    possible avalanches.

4. Small bark bettles bear a fungus that causes a disease of the
    Dutch elm tree.

5. Fashion designers sometimes copy the traditional dress of
    nomadic tribes.

6. Horizontal stripes on clothes emphasize heaviness and are
    shunned by stout people.

7. The high prices of new cars will continue to climb before they
    level off.

8. Sand painting, the ancient art of painting pictures with
    colored sand, was originated by American Indians for their
    traditional rituals.

9. Some elk from overpopulated herds in Yellowstone National Park
    have been exported to other parks and even to other countries.

10. Charcoal, first used as a filter in gas masks during the First
    World War, cleans the air in submarines and spacecraft and
    also filters automobile emissions.

Individual responses will vary. Encourage discussion of the differences.

1. prudent (1); careful (2); cautious (3)

2. perilous (3); dangerous (2); scary (1)

3. demanded (3); requested (2); wanted (1)

4. dislike (2); disapprove (1); detest (3)

5. like (3); adore (1); appreciate (2)

6. uncertain (1); insecure (2); desperate (3)

7. absurd (3); silly (1); preposterous (2)

8. talented (1); capable (3); competent (2)

9. quiet (3); restful (2); serene (1)

10. rile (3); peeve (2); annoy (1)

11. wither (2); languish (1); shrivel (3)

12. simple (3); naive (2); innocent (1)

13. impulsive (3); spontaneous (1); unconstrained (2)

14. famous (2); notorious (3); well-known (1)

15. aged (3); mellow (2); mature (1)

16. food (1); meat (2); victuals (3)

17. automobile (2); car (3); limousine (1)

18. singer (3); vocalist (2); virtuoso (1)

19. vulture (1); scavenger (2); buzzard (3)

20. boat (3); ship (2); liner (1)

21. lie (3); deception (1); falsehood (2)

22. visionary (1); dreamer (2); romancer (3)

23. illegal (2); unlawful (1); criminal (3)

24. ignoble (1); vile (3); disreputable (2)

25. request (1); solicit (2); beg (3)

Individual responses will vary. Encourage discussion of the differences.

1. force (2); compel (1); coerce (3)

2. miscellaneous (2); motley (3); assorted (1)

3. offensive (1); repulsive (2); revolting (3)

4. haggard (2); cadaverous (3); wasted (1)

5. redeem (1); aid (3); save (2)

6. part (1); separate (2); sever (3)

7. intentions (1); design (3); end (2)

8. ration (1); dole (3); pittance (2)

9. motive (2); incentive (1); inducement (3)

10. clothed (3); attired (1); dressed (2)

11. awkward (1); bungling (3); incompetent (2)

12. dress (2); frock (3); gown (1)

13. puny (3); little (2); small (1)

14. plea (1); argue (2); exhort (3)

15. angry (2); mad (1); wrathful (3)

16. resist (2); defy (3); oppose (1)

17. distinguished (2); noted (3); renowned (1)

18. wealthy (1); rich (2); opulent (3)

19. probity (1); candor (2); frankness (3)

20. horde (2); crowd (1); mob (3)

21. alarming (3); frightful (2); scary (1)

22. fat (3); obese (2); corpulent (1)

23. imitation (1); counterfeit (2); sham (3)

24. perseverance (1); obstinancy (3); doggedness (2)

25. merchandise (1); hawk (3); peddle (2)

17.3 Figurative Language

1. whirling sheets

2. bellowed and growled

3. cataracts

4. piles of cotton

5. beat down

6. black heads

7. deep muttering

8. accompaniment

9. to roll hoarsely

10. leaped out quivering

11. long rolling peal

17.4 Flowery Language

Individual responses will vary. The following are good possibilities.

1. We looked at the clouds in the sky.

2. Two handsome contestants competed in the Mr. Universe finals.

3. Many cardiologists advise against eating too many rich foods
    at dinner.

4. Elegant clothing often disguises aristocratic miserliness.

5. Many poets have been inspired by the vision of innocent
    children playing joyfully in green meadows.

6. In autumn farmers harvest their crops.

7. Marriage has become the object of much sociological research
    in academia.

8. Rafters down the Mississippi provide the nocturnal chorus of
    bullfrogs with a spirited audience.

9. The pastel clouds signaled the storm's end.

10. The mountain summits were covered with ice and snow.

17.5 Vocabulary

1. c

2. a

3. b

4. c

5. a

6. b

7. c

8. a

9. c

10. b

11. a

12. b

13. b

14. a

15. a

16. a

17. c

18. a

19. c

20. b

17.6 Vocabulary

1. a

2. c

3. b

4. c

5. b

6. c

7. a

8. b

9. a

10. a

11. c

12. b

13. b

14. a

15. a

16. b

17. a

18. c

19. b

20. a

18.1 Topic Sentences

If country music, like soul and Latin music, remains a securely
delineated subgenre within pop, there are signs of erosion of that
purity. The hope, as well as the fear, in Nashville these days is
the "crossover," or the leap of a country song onto the national pop
sales charts, and hence from relatively modest success to the millions to be made when the big pop AM stations all over the country
start playing and propagating a record. The hope is that a country
singer can reach that wider acclaim. The fear is that, in so doing,
the artist may dilute his style past recognizability. And, further,
there is fear that the process can work the other way--the supposed
country charts in recent years have often been topped by such
artists as John Denver, Olivia Newton-John, and Linda Ronstadt.
They may be singing outwardly country songs, but they are hardly
country in either their biographies or their links to Nashville
musical institutions. The whole crossover phenomenon provides an
obvious musical metaphor for Southern culture and its relation to
the rest of America: crossover success means recognition on a
national level even as the indigenous roots that nourish that
success are eroded.

Needless to say, many older forms of country music remain vital
parts of our folk culture today. What distinguishes them from main-
stream country and what helps assure their traditional purity is
their very freedom from commercialism. There are some established
country stars who consciously revert to the Anglo-American folk tra-
dition that underlies all country music.

But the many folk festivals around the country are full of
eager "string bands"--fiddle-dominated ensembles that trace their
ancestry back through the crudely amplified fiddle groups of the
Depression to the traditional country and mountain ensembles of the
nineteenth century. This music goes by a variety of overlapping
names--"mountain music," "old-timey music"--that often refer to
similar music with only minor regional variants. The best-known
form of such older music is bluegrass, popularized by Eric Weiss-
berg with his music for the film Deliverance. Bluegrass is actually of fairly recent invention, for all its debts to older forms of
folk-country, and its inventors, Bill Monroe and the Bluegrass Boys,
are still regaling audiences with their blend of quick-stepping
tempos, exuberant fiddle playing, and high, hard tenorizing. More
recently, Earl Scruggs, once the banjo-playing half of the Flatt and

Scruggs duo, has attempted to broaden bluegrass's appeal by allying
it with quasi-rock instrumentation.

                              --John Rockwell
                               "Blues, and Other Noises
                                in the Night"

Responses about controlling ideas will vary.

18.2 Topic Sentences

    <u>After a musical has opened in New York and has had the rare</u>
<u>privilege of getting unanimous raves from the critics, everyone from</u>
<u>the producers, writers, and directors right on down to the chorus</u>
<u>relaxes to bask in the sunlight of critical acceptance, public sup-</u>
<u>port, and financial gain.</u>

    <u>The dancers, especially, enjoy the hit in a strange sort of</u>
<u>way</u>. They immediately go back to the strenuous activity of daily
jazz and ballet classes, masochistically stretching and twisting in
order to stay in shape for auditions when this show eventually
closes. After the strenuous activity of daytime classes, the
theatre often becomes a place to rest up and recuperate for
tomorrow's classes. Out come the magazines, books, knitting, and
small change for poker games, and even possibly TV with the sound
turned way down; the whole thing takes on the atmosphere of a USO.

    <u>At this point the management, in the flush of success, decides</u>
<u>that it can afford an extra dancer to cover the possibility that</u>
<u>dancers will be out sick from time to time.</u>

                      --Bob Evans
                      "How to Get a Job as a
                      'Swing Dancer' in a Hit
                      Broadway Show"

Responses about controlling ideas will vary.

18.3 Paragraph Unity: Topic Sentences

The rationales for saving wild species, at the onset of the
movement several decades ago, were largely ethical, esthetic, and
ecological. These fundamental arguments have since been joined by
another, equally important one. We depend on our fellow species for
our material welfare, and ultimately for our future survival, in all
sorts of unsuspected ways. Conserving the planet's tropical areas
is especially important to realizing the utilitarian benefits of
wild species. Some 70 percent of the Earth's plants and animals
exist in the tropics, which means--by and large--in developing
nations. Third World leaders may be personally aware of the ethical
and esthetic values of wildlife, but they also recognize that it is
politically unfeasible for their impoverished populations to retain
space for rhinos, giraffes, and jaguars when millions of hungry
people lack land to grow their crops. If wildlife can "pay its way"
in the marketplace and make a local economic contribution, then
space may yet be found for threatened species.

Although some may view the utilitarian rationale for pre-
serving species as a narrow view of wildlife's true value, there
need not be a conflict between the consideration of a species' economic contributions and the belief that its continued existence needs
no justification. But faced with expanding human populations,
especially in developing nations, we must realize there is less and
less room for wildlife that exists for its own sake.

We use hundreds of products each day that owe their existence
to plants and animals. The ways in which wild species support our
daily welfare fall under three main headings: agriculture, medicine,
and industry.

                        --Norman Myers
                          "By Saving Wild Species,
                          We May Be Saving Ourselves"

Responses about controlling ideas will vary.

18.4 Topic Sentences

The crucial role of journalism in a democracy is to provide a common ground of knowledge and analysis, a meeting place for national debate: it is the link between people and institutions. Without the information provided by newspapers and TV, citizens would have little basis for deciding what to believe and whom to support. Just as a pervasive mistrust of police could cause a breakdown of order, a growing hostility to the press could sever the ligaments of a workable society.

Moreover, without a strong and trusted press, people would have almost no way to keep their government and other big institutions honest. Government, particularly the Federal Establishment, has vast powers to mislead the people and manage the news. Officials can conceal impending actions until their effects are irreversible. Other big institutions--corporations, unions, hospitals, police forces--prefer to cloak their decision-making process and their performance from the scrutiny of the public, whose lives may be deeply affected. And despite the passage of shield laws to protect journalists from having to reveal sources, they are regularly subpoenaed to testify about what they have reported.

Journalists became so aggressive partly because they knew, contrary to the widely held public view, that they were Davids fighting Goliaths. As the press itself grows into a more powerful institution, it must be careful how it uses its strength, whether it faces an ordinary individual or a President: the attempt to uncover can too easily turn into the impulse to tear apart.

Freedom of the press, like any other freedom, can be dangerous. But Thomas Jefferson, who suffered at the hands of journalists as much as any contemporary politician, insisted that protecting the press at its worst was an essential part of having the press be free.

> --William A. Henry, III
> "Journalism Under Fire"

Responses about controlling ideas will vary.

18.5 Digressive Sentences

A. 2

B. 2

C. 3, 4, 8

D. 2, 8

E. 4, 7

F. 2, 6

G. 2, 5

H. 3, 6

I. 5, 7

J. 2

K. 2

L. 5

M. 5

N. 3

O. 4

18.6 Transitions

When students complete a first draft, they consider the job of writing done--and their teachers too often agree. When professional writers complete a first draft, they usually feel that they are at the start of the writing process. When a draft is completed, the job of writing can begin.

That difference in attitude is the difference between amateur and professional, inexperience and experience, journeyman and craftsman. Peter F. Drucker, the prolific business writer, calls his first draft "the zero draft"--after that he can start counting. Most writers share the feeling that the first draft, and all of those which follow, are opportunities to discover what they have to say and how best they can say it.

To produce a progression of drafts, each of which says more and says it more clearly, the writer has to develop a special kind of reading skill. In school we are taught to decode what appears on the page as finished writing. Writers, however, face a different category of possibility and responsibility when they read their own drafts. To them the words on the page are never finished. Each can be changed and rearranged, can set off a chain reaction of confusion or clarified meaning. This is a different kind of reading which is possibly more difficult and certainly more exciting.

--Donald Murray
"The Maker's Eye: Revising
Your Own Manuscripts"

To the instructor:

Instructors' appraisals are an invaluable source of information for authors and publishers in planning future editions of books. In order to meet the changing needs of instructors and students in the next edition of <u>PRACTICAL ENGLISH WORKBOOK</u>, it would be helpful to us if you would send us your evaluation of the text. Please complete this questionnaire and mail it to Floyd C. Watkins/William B. Dillingham/John T. Hiers, c/o Marketing Services, College Division, Houghton Mifflin Company, One Beacon Street, Boston, MA 02108.

1. Please describe your school briefly (e.g., two-year, four-year, university, private, state): _____
    _____

2. Title of the course(s) in which you used this book:
    _____

3. Which text, if any, did you use in this course previously?
    _____

4. To what extent did PRACTICAL ENGLISH WORKBOOK, Third Edition, meet the needs of your course?

    __completely __to a great extent __fairly well __poorly

5. Did you assign every chapter of the book? ___yes ___no
    If no, indicate which chapters you did not assign:
    _____

6. Which chapters did you find especially helpful, and why?
    _____
    _____
    _____

7. Are there any chapters that would be made more helpful by substantial revision? Please note the changes you would advise:
    _____
    _____
    _____
    _____

8. Did you find the exercises throughout the text helpful? Were there enough exercises? _____
    _____
    _____

9. Please feel free to make any further comments: _____
    _____
    _____
    _____
    _____